ANIMAL FAMILIES

WOLVES
LIFE IN THE PACK

Willow Clark

PowerKiDS
press
New York

Published in 2011 by The Rosen Publishing Group, Inc.
29 East 21st Street, New York, NY 10010

First Edition

Editor: Jennifer Way
Book Design: Julio Gil

Photo Credits: Cover, p. 10–11 Jupiterimages/Liquidlibrary/Thinkstock; back cover © www.iStockphoto.com/Kristijan Hranisavljevic; pp. 5, 24 (bottom left) Comstock Images/Thinkstock; pp. 7, 21, 23, 24 (top right) Shutterstock.com; pp. 9, 17 (main, inset) iStockphoto/Thinkstock; pp. 13, 19, 24 (bottom right) Jupiterimages/Photos.com/Thinkstock; pp. 15, 24 (top left) Tom Brakefield/Stockbyte/Thinkstock; p. 17 Tom Brakefield/Getty Images.

Library of Congress Cataloging-in-Publication Data

Clark, Willow.
  Wolves : life in the pack / by Willow Clark. — 1st ed.
    p. cm. — (Animal families)
  Includes index.
  ISBN 978-1-4488-2515-8 (library binding) — ISBN 978-1-4488-2616-2 (pbk.) —
ISBN 978-1-4488-3047-3 (6-pack)
  1. Wolves—Juvenile literature. 2. Familial behavior in animals—Juvenile literature. I. Title.
  QL737.C22C565 2011
  599.773—dc22

2010019394

Manufactured in the United States of America

CPSIA Compliance Information: Batch #WW11PK: For Further Information contact Rosen Publishing, New York, New York at 1-800-237-9932

CONTENTS

Wolves live together in a family group, called a **pack**.

A wolf pack has a pair of adult wolves that are **mates**.

Each pack member has a place within the pack. The leader is the strongest male.

Baby wolves are called **pups**. The pups are part of the pack, too.

Other adult wolves may join the pack. They must follow the leader.

13

Wolves make different sounds to talk to each other. They whine, growl, bark, and **howl**.

A wolf pack works together to hunt. Wolves hunt deer, elks, moose, and other animals.

Deer

The pack also works together to raise the pups.

The pups play a lot. Playing helps them learn about life in the pack.

Wolves make their homes in dens. A den is often a hole in the ground.

23

Words to Know

howl

mates

pack

pups

Index

Web Sites

Due to the changing nature of Internet links, PowerKids Press has developed an online list of Web sites related to the subject of this book. This site is updated regularly. Please use this link to access the list:
www.powerkidslinks.com/afam/wolves/